To the people who left a mark on my heart.

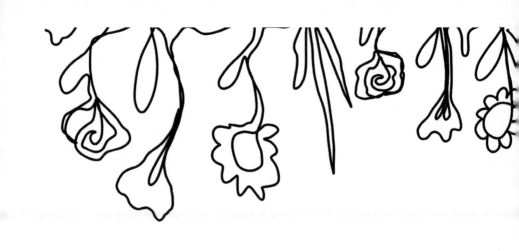

What do my flower beds represent?

The poor weeping flowers that sat across from me

What are they showing?

I thought these places were meant to be bright and colourful

But mine show the opposite.

When will they bloom again.

When will my flower beds be joyous and no longer be in the dark?

When will the flowers stop feeling this pain that has been placed upon us.

When will the men stop stamping on my poor wounded flowers.

When will I see them thrive once again.

The roots rot

You forgot

Once again

When will I be able to trust

For you not to forget

That these flowers I have

Need to be cared for

Need to be loved

But you will forget

Once's again

So the roots will rot

I buried you. In the garden of my mind. Under the flower beds of memories. Under all the different feelings I feel. However I have to bury you. Even though you haunt my mind. The memories seep through the soil. Killing away the flowers. Killing away a part of me. A healthy part. You rot my brain. Filling me with so many difficult emotions. The emotions that I had for you. I loved you once but you decided to torture me. Only you will be able to know I am really talking about you.

I bury you in the rows of flowers hoping that they will cover what little memory I have of you. The memory of you touching my skin. The kisses along my back. The memories where I was asleep to feel you where I did not want to feel you in those moments. The good and bad. The moment on the beach when we concluded it was over after months and months even those these bad things happened. 4 months or even 5 months of my life that felt like it lasted a decade. I bury these under the flower beds of memories to let you decay with out a trace.

A garden

Of hope

I see you my love

There you stand it feels so far.

I cannot reach you

Please find me one day

A heavy heart I lay out for you

You exam each petal with your admiring eyes

Then gone

As you promised you wouldn't

Though you did come back and showed me yours

I look at the petals in you hands

To show that we can become one

I lived with the pain once again

Watching every part of me die.

You all placed you mark on my flowers.

You thorn's damage me.

Suffocate my mind.

You all used and abused a beautiful garden that I wanted to keep.

Each one coming into my life and destroying a flower.

My innocents.

My heart.

My home.

You all destroyed a part of me that I wanted to keep.

My flowers weep for you

They beg for your touch

Your brightness

To help them to survive

They droop in sadness

As you walk on by

I need you

They need you

Our existence is for you

Rejection causes the trees the shake

                                    And the flowers start to close

Don't wound them please

                I will try my hardest to not let my mind wonder

About the things that could of been

              As your rejection made the leaves fall from tree

Realising that I have to contain this feeling

                           Now it takes an effect

They may not leave

                           So the trees heal once again

Guilty

A feeling that my wild blooms mourn

Guilty

A feeling of betrayal

Guilty

Flash backs appear like leaves falling from the tree

Guilty

Please I promise I didn't mean to

Guilty

It's all my fault

Guilty

This will haunt me

Wild blooms

They feel so good

They thrive in the feelings that are positive

But die when the bad memories appear

My wild blooms

Such a blessing on my soul

They are my wild blooms

Finally maybe they live like I will too

Your hands are the like poisonous ivy

They burn across my skin

Leaving their torturous mark

I feel them sting as I am asleep

Wakes me in a panic

Reminds me of where you have been

But I am safe now as I gaze across to my wild flower

However the deadly ivy still lingers

Reminding me of what you did

Are you the Lilly in my life

The one that fills my lungs

Leaving me breathless

Is that a good or bad thing

Or are you doing this to hurt me

The pollen from your Lilly garden kills me

So slowly

As I suffocate seeing you

These lilies will be the death of me

Not all hope is lost

When the sun flowers bloom

Reminding me all the happiness which life has given me

They absorb all the sun light that I can give

My sun flower

I will always love you

The breeze flows through the grass

The feeling of being calm

The blue sky's are refreshing

Helping with clearing my mind

The flowers are feeling free

And my garden is open

Welcome to my home

The flowers are so different

Some stay strong

And some just die

They are affected by the world around me

I try my hardest to protect them

But sometimes I fail

I feel so useless

I try my hardest to keep you alive

And all I can keep doing is trying

My flowers are so different

I feel you close to me

My flowers bloom

I feel so alone

My flowers die

I need to share air with you

But I become obsessed

I can't have you

But I need you

How I love that you bring the sunshine

My flowers thrive when I see you

I feel amazing as you walk through

Making me breathless

I cannot live without you

Nor can the flowers

We need your rays of sunshine

To keep living

Night after night

I watch the wounds heal

My garden finally grows strong

However there are still the scars left behind

The beautiful white roses are left

Showing how far I have come

They lay upon my skin

And I will admire them

And keep admiring

All through my life

You cross my garden

Bringing me heart ache

You told my flowers to many promises

That you would protect them.

That you would help them heal.

You said if any one hurt the flowers that you would be there
no matter what.

So I tell you what happened

You look down on the flowers

And left

You chose the one who hurt my flowers

Who destroyed my garden

You chose not to keep your promises

Now my flowers are dead

With no one to protect them

Because you left

Sometimes I feel like I truly forgotten what it feels like to be in love.

Those times at night with deep thoughts.

That are buried deep in the garden.

Will I ever be able to love again?

Have I ever been able to love?

After the men who have stolen from my garden and took advantage of all my beautiful flowers.

Am I really in love anymore?

Or is it a feeling of obsession?

Or just the need for someone rather than being in love

Do I really fall in love anymore?

Can I even love after what's happened?

Is this love anymore.

Flowers grow

The same way my feelings do for
you

So here you go

I admit to it all

I love you

Forever you walk across my garden

I watch you admiringly

You care for each flower

Watering each one

Talking to them all

Is this what love feels like

I admire you more

As you tend to my garden

Not at a single point did you get scared

Not at a single point did you think this is to much

You embrace my garden

Including the weeds

As I watch you cross the garden

And think

I have two roses

I want to love both

But they don't work in the same soil

One red

One white

I try to look after each one

But one will always weep

I'm never feeling good enough

As they both fight to stay in my garden

I sit and think

I love you both

Please I need you both

One red

One white

In my garden lays the truth

The truth of what really happened

How his thorns suffocated my flowers

How another trampled on the place where happiness grows

The other took my blue bells

Replacing them with dark destroying weeds

How you would believe that these people wouldn't hurt a soul

How I believed they wouldn't hurt my garden

Now my garden suffered

I'll show you

My weeds that happiness can thrive

Even in the darkest of places

We need the rain

To help the garden grow

Those weeping clouds will help the other things in need

They help the flowers bud

The grass will go green

The rain clouds with help all those small things

It's okay to cry clouds

The sunshine always comes after

So let it go

Let the feelings finally be free

Let those tears fall

As it helps everything grow

To this day men have cursed upon my garden. Leaving their weeds of torture. The weeds they leave in my brain. Determine the way I grow. Determine the way I should be, how I should act, the way I should respond to an action. However I cannot accept what the weeds have done to my garden. Those men hurt me in ways no human should be hurt. The emotional, physical and mental torture they each put upon me.

You have shaped who I am today. I have accepted my true colours. The colours you didn't like. That none of you liked. No longer skinny. No longer bleach blonde. No longer dressing in a way to please you. No longer studying science like you wanted. I rebelled against all your wishes. Slowly recovering from the torturous memories you placed on me. Becoming a person who lives for themselves rather than someone else.

I can't do this alone

Please I need you

Help me save my garden

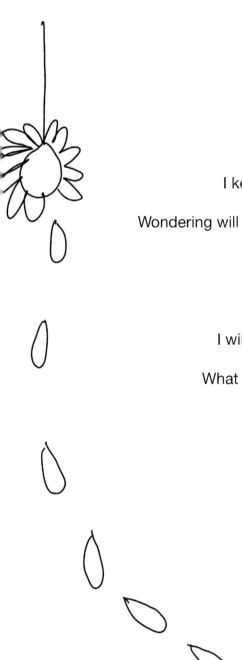

Picking at  the petals

I sit and wonder

They love me

They love me not

I keep picking at the petals

Wondering will there ever be an answer

They love me

They love me not

I will keep picking till I know

What will the answer ever be?

So many different flowers

Representing a different time

The blue bells sharing memories of sorrow

The sun flower showing memories of happiness

My roses I share to my loved ones

So many flowers to admire

So many more to grow

He brings me flowers

To fill my garden

He makes me  feel so happy

He brings me flowers

To build more memories

He always bring me flowers

When I'm feeling cloudy

He will bring me flowers

To say sorry

He always bring me flowers

Is this real

The world beyond

I don't want to leave my safe place

I don't want to leave my garden

I've been hurt too much

From the outside world

My garden is where I want to be

No place else

Sometimes I sit in my garden alone

Sometimes I need to be alone

The world is too over whelming

But my garden is safe

From all the harm that the world brings

I sit alone in my garden

Embracing the peace

As the world outside

Breaks me in pieces

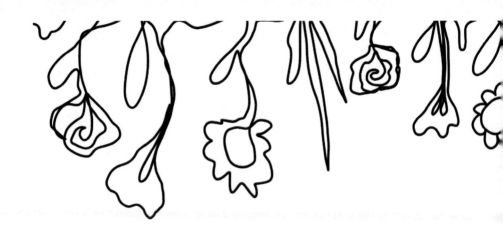

Where the flowers grow you live. In my heart you thrive. But in my mind you died. The thoughts drown you out. I can't love you. Not anymore. It hurts the flowers to much. Look at them weep. I can't love you anymore. Maybe listening to my brain might do me some good. You live in the soil now. Helping the flowers carry on. As my brain can't comprehend the pain no longer. The distance between us grew like the ivy on my house. We can no longer hold on to something that doest exist anymore. As my heart aches for you my brains shuts down. The garden will look after you now. The garden will keep the memory of you living as my brain forgets the sound of your voice. My garden will take care of you my love.

I promise

Sat alone

Surrounded by flowers

Drowned by thoughts

I need you

But who

My garden

My love

My family

My enemies

My abusers

Who do I need?

Drown me flowers

As you are so pretty

Maybe I rest in peace

Knowing

I tried

I stare at the stars at night

Laid out across the grass

In my garden

Looking to my side

Is it you that I'm looking at

Do you know it's you who I'm looking at

Our hands connect together

Like the roots of a plant becoming intertwined

We stare at the sky we share

Counting the stars

Do you know its you I'm after

Our lips drew closer

Like two asteroids colliding

Stare back at the stars

Do we really want this

Do you know its you who I look at

Laid across my garden

A bench where I sit

Pondering how I could fix things

Is the garden patch we share worth saving

Should I keep going with this

Will you be there

Or am I doing this alone again

This is our garden

That needs both our love

However I never see you

I never hear your voice anymore

So I sit a ponder

Is this worth keeping

Feeling you warm breath across my neck

Making the flowers open wide

Your kisses feed me and my garden

Your intimacy is what we crave

I need to feel you close

Please come near

Help me keep this garden alive

I crave your attention

Give me your love

I let you in

To my garden and you will see

We need you

I need you

Your hands feel like the soft petals from roses

Your kisses fill the empty patches in my garden

Your smell fills the air

Running my hands through your hair like I do when I'm sat
on the grass

Take a seat my love

Let me take care of you

Let my flowers suffocate you in love and lust

Let me worship you

I appreciate you more

So come to my garden

Let me love you

Another year.

Just another year.

Realising I am still here.

Reminding myself all the reason I should stay alive.

After it all.

All the things I saw this year.

Waiting for them to trigger something in my mind.

Waiting for me to go crazy.

Another year of loss and gain.

Lost a friend and another one comes home.

He comes home to me.

Feeling happy but also so much guilt.

Feel like I don't deserve any of this.

Another year but covid seems that it will never disappear.

Another year and I decided fuck it.

I do whatever I want.

Another year and the roller coaster seems like it never end.

Another year I can't think about what will happen in the next one.

Here I am still breathing and still living another year.

Fill my mind with all your wild blooms

Fill me with every flower you own

I want to know every part of you

And your garden

Let me in

As I let you into mine

I like to know

How you grow such beautiful plants

As mine is filled with weeds

Your mind is so interesting

Just let me in

I keep you safe in my garden

A place where my flowers grow.

They look after you

Keeping every part of your existence in my mind

Just lay there and keep calm

As they grow over you

Keeping every part of you alive

You voice

your smell

Your hair

And you lips

Everything that makes you

I promise you my love

Your safe with them

The weeds consume me sometimes

To overwhelmed to deal with

They make so you feel so alone

Destroying all things beautiful

However,

Sometimes there is hope

That maybe a person

Or a moment

Where the weeds feel small

And the flowers flourish

So I tell myself

The weeds may consume me

But it doesn't mean, they are me.

This garden feels endless

As it keeps growing

I find new gates, mountains, fields and rivers

Learning all new things

As a new memory is made a flower grows

This garden feels endless

Leaves me wondering

Will there ever be an end

An end to this garden

My garden

Thank you

Keep growing

I need you

This book was written with inspiration from a series of paintings I did in 2022.

I wanted to use the work to represent my trauma and how it has affected me as an individual. The work is subject to my own experience, not generalised to everyone else. I wanted to explore and process the things I have been through emotionally and creatively. The text gives an idea of what happened, but the painting disrupts that. Linking back to feelings of disassociation and confusion. The effects of what trauma has had on me. I wanted to create work that people can experience and get lost in but also understand what happened to me and how I have been affected by these traumatic experiences.

This series of paintings led me to write loads and loads of feelings that I have suppressed over my years. This time round I want the words to be read. I want to be able to gain an understanding from what I have felt after what's happened to me. We are all human and all have complexed feelings. This is what I wanted to achieve with this book.

The next couple of pages are images from the work I created

Chloe Beth

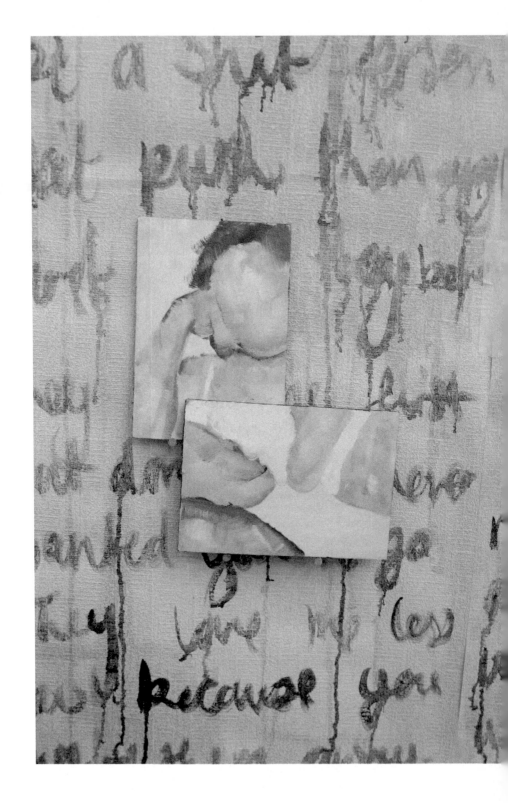

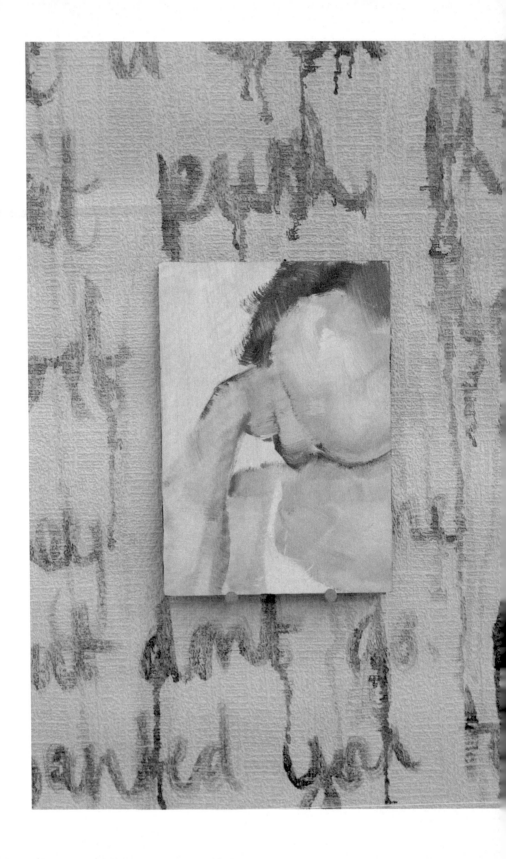

Thank you

Printed in Great Britain
by Amazon

85976442R00047

# Welcome to my garden. Please treat with respect and care.

ISBN 9798844432378

# *$elf*
# PUBLISHED
# MILLIONAIRE

The **Step-By-Step** Guide To Writing, Publishing
and Marketing Your First Book

## JOSEPH ALEXANDER
## & TIM PETTINGALE